D1064844

# MISSION TO MARS

# MARS ROVERS

### BY
### JOHN HAMILTON

**Abdo & Daughters**
An imprint of Abdo Publishing | abdopublishing.com

**abdopublishing.com**

Published by Abdo Publishing, a division of ABDO, PO Box 398166, Minneapolis, Minnesota 55439. Copyright © 2019 by Abdo Consulting Group, Inc. International copyrights reserved in all countries. No part of this book may be reproduced in any form without written permission from the publisher. Abdo & Daughters™ is a trademark and logo of Abdo Publishing.

Printed in the United States of America, North Mankato, Minnesota.
062018
092018

THIS BOOK CONTAINS RECYCLED MATERIALS

**Editor:** Sue Hamilton
**Copy Editor:** Bridget O'Brien
**Graphic Design:** Sue Hamilton
**Cover Design:** Candice Keimig and Pakou Moua
**Cover Photo:** iStock
**Interior Images:** All Images NASA, except: European Space Agency-pg 43; Granger-pg 11; Science Source-pg 13; Steam Community-pg 6.

Library of Congress Control Number: 2017963899
Publisher's Cataloging-in-Publication Data
Names: Hamilton, John, author.
Title: Mars rovers / by John Hamilton.
Description: Minneapolis, Minnesota : Abdo Publishing, 2019. | Series: Mission to Mars | Includes online resources and index.
Identifiers: ISBN 9781532115967 (lib.bdg.) | ISBN 9781532156892 (ebook)
Subjects: LCSH: Mars (Planet)--Exploration--Equipment and supplies--Juvenile literature. | Mars (Planet)--Exploration--Juvenile literature.
Classification: DDC 523.43--dc23

# CONTENTS

# JOURNEY ACROSS AN ALIEN WORLD

Humans first landed robotic spacecraft on the surface of Mars during the 1970s. Scientists gathered a huge amount of data from these stationary machines. However, to learn more about the Red Planet, a new generation of science laboratories was launched. They were packed with experiments to test Mars's atmosphere and soil. They bristled with cameras to capture images of the alien landscape. Most importantly, they could move across the Martian surface. Scientists were no longer stuck in one spot. These rovers travelled across Mars on missions that often lasted for years.

NASA's Curiosity rover landed on Mars on August 6, 2012. Packed with a drill, chemistry labs, and 17 cameras, the car-sized rover was designed to discover evidence of ancient waterways, and to determine whether life may have once existed on the Red Planet.

# SOJOURNER

In the mid-20th century, the United States and the Soviet Union were locked in the Space Race with each other. In 1971, the Soviet Union tried to land twin probes on Mars. They were part of the Mars 2 and Mars 3 missions. For the first time, these landers included something new: small rovers that could explore the Martian surface.

The Soviet machines were called the Prop-M rovers. About the same size as modern video game consoles, they had moveable metal skis on the bottom. They used the skis to shuffle along the surface. They could also detect and avoid obstacles. Unfortunately, both of the Soviet landers failed. The rovers never had a chance to perform their mission. Mars 2 crashed on the surface, and Mars 3 lost contact with Earth within minutes after landing.

The Soviet Union's twin probes, Mars 2 and Mars 3, included small rovers called Prop-M. With moveable metal skis on the bottom, they were designed to explore the surface of Mars.

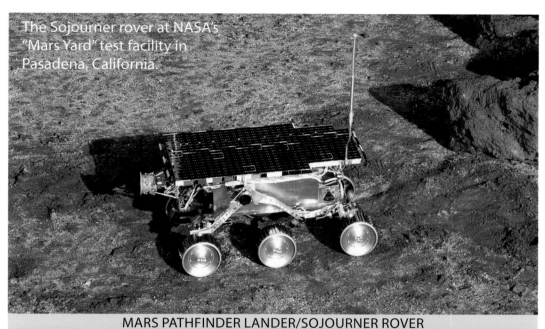

The Sojourner rover at NASA's "Mars Yard" test facility in Pasadena, California.

| MARS PATHFINDER LANDER/SOJOURNER ROVER | | | |
|---|---|---|---|
| Mission: | Mars lander/rover | Mars Touchdown: | July 4, 1997 |
| Launch: | December 4, 1996 | Mission End: | September 27, 1997 |
| Launch Vehicle: | Delta II | Spacecraft weight (mass): | 1,020 pounds  (463 kg) |

In 1997, the United States returned to Mars. More than two decades had passed since NASA had sent the Viking landers to the Red Planet. The new lander's name was Pathfinder. Piggybacking on Pathfinder was a six-wheeled, microwave-oven-sized rover called Sojourner. (The rover was named after the African American Civil War abolitionist Sojourner Truth. The word sojourner means "traveler.")

Pathfinder was part of NASA's Discovery Program. Its motto was "better, faster, cheaper." Each mission was designed to be built quickly and for relatively little money (for a spacecraft). Pathfinder had a simple mission: test the Sojourner rover in the cold, hostile environment of Mars.

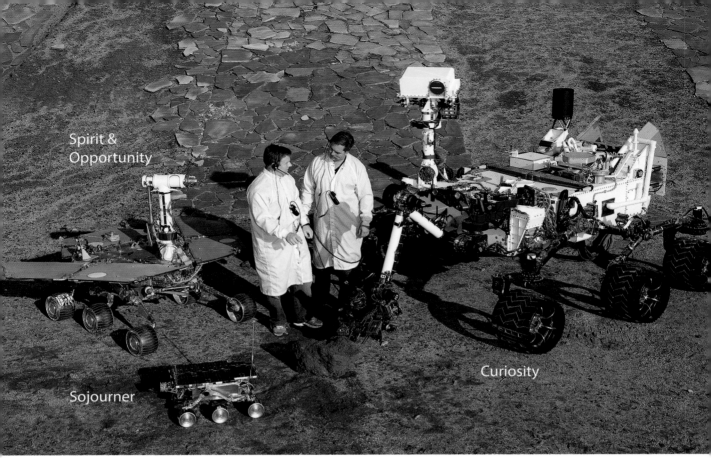

Spirit &
Opportunity

Sojourner

Curiosity

NASA engineers stand by duplicates of three generations of rovers.
Sojourner was much smaller than future generations, but it accomplished
a lot. Sojourner spent 83 days of a planned seven-day mission exploring the
Martian terrain, acquiring images, and taking chemical, atmospheric, and
other measurements.

The Sojourner rover measured about 2 feet (.6 m) long, 1.5 feet
(.45 m) wide, and 1 foot (.3 m) high. It weighed 23 pounds (10.4 kg). The
rover had cleats on each of its six wheels to give it traction in the dusty
Martian soil. Its top speed was about 2 feet per minute (.6 m/min).

A solar panel on the rover's roof provided power, while five lasers
helped controllers on Earth identify and avoid obstacles. Two small,
front-mounted black-and-white cameras took stereo pictures. A color
camera was in back. An alpha proton X-ray spectrometer identified
the kinds of rocks and soil Sojourner would discover on its mission.

Sojourner got around the Martian landscape with the help of six aluminum wheels. Each had stainless steel treads and cleats for maximum traction, and were 5 inches (13 cm) in diameter. The robotic rover's rocker-bogie suspension gave the wheels great stability, which was important for the uneven terrain it would encounter. Sojourner could even climb over rocks 8 inches (20 cm) high if necessary. Normally, however, it would use a laser system to detect and avoid large obstacles.

The Sojourner rover had six wheels with stainless steel treads and cleats for maximum traction. The rover's rocker-bogie suspension allowed it to go over rock-filled and uneven terrain.

# PATHFINDER AND SOJOURNER REACH MARS

Pathfinder blasts off toward Mars atop a Delta II rocket.

O n December 4, 1996, the Pathfinder lander, with Sojourner nestled safely within, blasted off from Florida's Cape Canaveral Air Force Station atop a powerful Delta II rocket. The spacecraft began a long, arching path to catch up with Mars on its orbit around the Sun. On July 4, 1997, after a trip of more than 300 million miles (483 million km), it reached its destination. Operating completely on its own, it entered the Red Planet's outer atmosphere at about 16,000 miles per hour (25,750 kph).

Pathfinder, slowed by a huge parachute and retrorockets, descends to Mars.

Aerobraking through the thin atmosphere helped Pathfinder slow down to about 800 miles per hour (1,287 kph). Protected by a heat shield, the spacecraft blazed a fiery trail across the pink Martian sky.

Several miles above the surface, a huge, 36-foot (11-m) -diameter parachute opened, slowing the spacecraft down to about 160 miles per hour (257 kph). A few seconds later, the heat shield was discarded.

Directly below Pathfinder lay its target: Ares Vallis. It was a wide floodplain at the mouth of a major canyon system. At one time, floodwaters equal to all five of Earth's Great Lakes washed through this now-dry valley. Geologists expected to find all kinds of rocks strewn over the landscape.

Eighty seconds from touchdown, about 3 miles (4.8 km) from the surface, the main lander was quickly winched down from the rocket pack. It dangled on a 65-foot (20-m) -long tether made of tough Kevlar fabric. The lander used radar to measure its distance from the surface. Eight seconds before landing, sets of large airbags were rapidly inflated that protected the precious cargo inside. Braking rockets fired briefly, and the tether was released. Pathfinder free-fell to the surface, 70 feet (21 m) below. It impacted at a speed of about 40 miles per hour (64 kph).

Engineers test the inflated airbags that will surround and protect Pathfinder as it drops to the Mars surface.

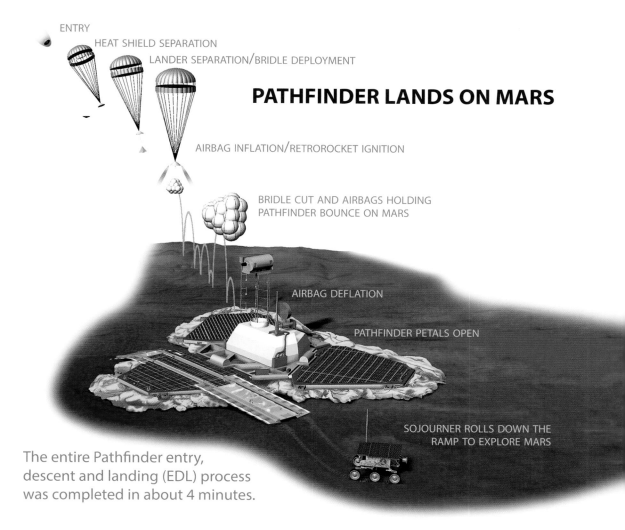

ENTRY

HEAT SHIELD SEPARATION

LANDER SEPARATION/BRIDLE DEPLOYMENT

# PATHFINDER LANDS ON MARS

AIRBAG INFLATION/RETROROCKET IGNITION

BRIDLE CUT AND AIRBAGS HOLDING
PATHFINDER BOUNCE ON MARS

AIRBAG DEFLATION

PATHFINDER PETALS OPEN

SOJOURNER ROLLS DOWN THE
RAMP TO EXPLORE MARS

The entire Pathfinder entry,
descent and landing (EDL) process
was completed in about 4 minutes.

When the airbag-encased spacecraft hit, it bounced nearly
45 feet (14 m) high, then fell to the ground again. It bounced at least
15 times, finally settling to a stop on the frigid plain of Ares Vallis.

For the first time in 21 years, humans had made their mark on
Mars once again. Scientists at NASA's Jet Propulsion Laboratory
(JPL), who were overseeing the mission, were overjoyed.

Pathfinder had landed at about 3:00 a.m. on Mars. The airbags
were slowly deflated, and the lander's three solar panels opened like
a big metallic flower. When dawn struck, rays from the Sun began
powering the probe's instruments.

# THE FIRST ROVER TO EXPLORE MARS

After landing on Mars, Pathfinder sent its first photos of the alien landscape that morning. The detailed images were stunning. The scene looked like it was from the American Southwest, but without cacti or sagebrush.

The rust-colored Martian soil was littered with rocks and boulders of every shape and size. The geologists on the NASA team were thrilled. In the distance, under a salmon-colored sky, were two tall hills. They were later named Twin Peaks.

NASA announced that it had renamed the lander the Carl Sagan Memorial Station, after the popular astronomer Carl Sagan. He had died earlier in 1997. His work had greatly helped in the push to send spacecraft to Mars. On that first day, the lander sent a weather report. The temperature was a numbing -64 degrees Fahrenheit (-53° C). The spacecraft was expected to withstand such conditions for about 30 Martian days (called sols).

Pathfinder took a photo of Sojourner in its traveling position, before the rover unfolded and prepared to move to the surface of Mars.

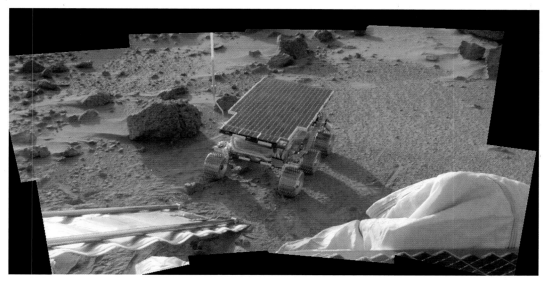

Late in the day on Sol 2, Sojourner was instructed to roll down the Pathfinder ramp and wait. Eight images were combined to let Earth operators know what surrounded the newly deployed rover, before it moved across the Martian surface.

On Sol 2, it was the Sojourner rover's turn to shine. To move around on the surface of Mars, Sojourner received its instructions from controllers back on Earth. But operating Sojourner was nothing like playing with a radio-controlled car or helicopter. During its mission, Earth and Mars would be 119 million miles (192 million km) apart. Radio signals traveling at the speed of light would take about 11 minutes to get to Mars. The rover's controllers had to give instructions that were slow and deliberate. If something went wrong, they couldn't react in time to save the little rover.

Sojourner rolled down a steep ramp toward the surface of Mars. The process took most of the day. Controllers at JPL were cautious because so many things could go wrong. The small rover could tip, or get a wheel stuck on the edge of the ramp, or even get tangled in the deflated fabric of the lander's airbags.

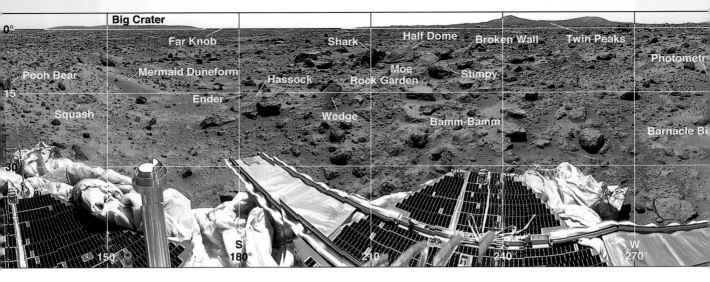

Big Crater
Far Knob
Shark
Half Dome
Broken Wall
Twin Peaks
Pooh Bear
Mermaid Duneform
Moe
Stimpy
Photometr
Hassock
Rock Garden
Ender
Squash
Wedge
Bamm-Bamm
Barnacle Bi
0°
15
30
S
180°
150
210°
240
W
270°

By the end of Sol 2, Sojourner had all six wheels planted firmly on Martian soil. Its first task was to sniff the dirt and nearby rocks with its alpha proton X-ray spectrometer. For 10 hours it sent data to the lander, which relayed the information back to Earth.

In the following days, Sojourner moved to investigate rocks around the landing site, including a boulder called Yogi. Sometimes Sojourner ran across large rocks, but its six metal-cleated wheels moved independently of each other, which usually kept it from getting stuck.

Sojourner photographed Yogi, the large rock in the center, on Sol 70. Much of Yogi in this image could not be seen from the lander. Sojourner's treadmarks and its left front wheel are seen in the photo.

Sojourner analyzed the Martian rocks and soil and took pictures. It never roamed more than about 30 feet (9 m) from the Carl Sagan Memorial Station (Pathfinder), but there was plenty to study. A huge flood had clearly washed across this part of the planet long ago. The rocks were volcanically formed, but many had to have come from other parts of the planet during the flood. But where had all the water gone? That question would have to be answered by future missions.

The Carl Sagan Memorial Station (Pathfinder) was designed to last 30 days. Sojourner was expected to last just 7 days. However, both machines kept working for many extra weeks. Finally, on September 27, 1997, the lander sent its last message from Mars. It had fallen victim to the planet's harsh conditions.

By mission's end, the lander had sent back more than 16,000 images, plus 550 images from Sojourner. It also sent more than 15 chemical analyses of rocks, plus data about Mars's weather patterns. The mission also proved that the new technology it used could work on Mars. Future spacecraft builders could learn from its success.

# SPIRIT AND OPPORTUNITY

After the success of the 1997 Pathfinder mission, NASA prepared to return to the Martian surface. This time, twin rovers would explore the Red Planet. The mission of the Mars Exploration Rovers (MER) program was to look for evidence of water in the planet's distant past. The rovers would do this by analyzing the rocks and soil they encountered.

NASA's MER program patch.

Some rocks and minerals are formed only in the presence of water.

By finding clues to past water, scientists could tell what kind of wet environments existed on ancient Mars. Water is a necessary ingredient for life as we know it. NASA hoped to find out if life could have sprung from Mars long ago.

The two MER program rovers were named Spirit and Opportunity. The names were chosen from a student essay contest that had almost 10,000 entries. Spirit's lander was named Columbia Memorial Station. Opportunity's lander was named Challenger Memorial Station. They were named in honor of destroyed space shuttles Columbia (2003) and Challenger (1986) and the heroic astronauts who died in the tragedies.

| MARS EXPLORATION ROVERS | | |
|---|---|---|
| Mission: Mars rovers | Mars Touchdown: Spirit: Jan. 4, 2004 | |
| Launch: Spirit: June 10, 2003 | Opportunity: Jan. 25, 2004 | |
| Opportunity: July 7, 2003 | Mission End: Spirit: March 22, 2010 | |
| Launch Vehicles: Delta II | Opportunity: Continuing | |
| | Spacecraft weight (mass) rover only: 384 pounds (174 kg) | |

The golf-cart-sized rovers were designed and built at NASA's Jet Propulsion Laboratory in Pasadena, California. During their construction, scientists studied high-resolution images of Mars taken by the Mars Global Surveyor and Mars Odyssey orbiters. They chose two landing sites on roughly opposite sides of the planet. Each site seemed promising. The Spirit rover would be going to Gusev Crater, a 103-mile (166-km) -wide basin that may once have held a lake. Opportunity would land in a broad plain called Meridiani Planum. Orbiter images hinted that it may also have had a watery past.

Just before launch, NASA technicians work on Opportunity inside its lander.

Spirit and Opportunity borrowed many design ideas from the Pathfinder mission. Each rover had six wheels and used rocker-bogie suspensions. This would allow them to roll over obstacles and climb steep hills. Other similarities to Pathfinder included airbags to cushion landing on the surface and using solar panels for power. The solar panels were mounted on "wings" that unfolded on the top of each rover.

Spirit and Opportunity were about 17 times heavier than the Sojourner rover. Sojourner's host, the Pathfinder lander, housed heavy communications equipment for contacting Earth, plus cameras and computers. Spirit and Opportunity carried all that equipment themselves. Their landers were built to protect them in flight. Once on the ground, the landers would unfold. The rovers would roll down a ramp onto the Martian surface, and the landers' mission would be over.

Spirit lifted off from Florida's Cape Canaveral Air Force Station on June 10, 2003. Opportunity followed on July 7, 2003. Each rover was tightly packed inside its lander. They survived dangerous solar flares during their six-month journeys through deep space.

Spirit launched on a Delta II rocket on June 10, 2003.

Spirit was the first to arrive at Mars. On January 4, 2004, the spacecraft hit the Martian atmosphere. As tremendous friction from the air slowed the lander down, a heat shield protected the rover inside. Acting on its own, it released a parachute. A few minutes later, the heat shield was released, and the rover was winched down on a 65-foot (20-m) tether. The lander used radar-guided retrorockets to slow the descent even more. The airbags around the rover inflated, and the tether was cut 40 feet (12 m) from the surface.

Protected by the airbags, Spirit hit the ground. It rolled and bounced 28 times before finally coming to a rest inside Gusev Crater. It was a near-perfect landing. After traveling 303 million miles (488 million km), Spirit was ready to begin its mission.

Right after touchdown, the lander retracted its airbags and opened its petals. Spirit unfolded its solar arrays and raised its camera mast, ready to roll onto Mars.

# CRATERS AND DUST DEVILS

After Spirit touched down inside Gusev Crater, the lander's side panels unfolded. Winches and cables retracted the airbags. Spirit used one of the side panels as a ramp to slowly roll down to the planet surface. Its cameras took pictures of the surrounding area. High-resolution panoramic images amazed scientists on Earth. The landscape was mostly flat, and strewn with small rocks.

Spirit (bottom left corner) takes photos of its protective lander shortly after arriving on Mars. The Columbia Memorial Station, or "empty nest," rests at Gusev Crater.

Spirit's camera shadow produces a "selfie," as the rover explores Mars.

For the first couple of weeks, Spirit slowly roamed around the landing site. It took photos and analyzed the area's geology. Scientists were disappointed in one of the earliest discoveries. Gusev Crater was filled with volcanic rock, which was mostly basalt. Orbiter images made scientists believe the area was once flooded with water, which is why Spirit was sent there in the first place. If that were true, then later volcanic lava flows had covered up any hint of a life-supporting environment long ago.

A computer glitch struck Spirit during its third week on Mars. As computer experts on Earth worked on the problem, the Opportunity rover arrived. It landed safely at Meridiani Planum on January 25, 2004. After bouncing 26 times on its airbags, it came to rest in a shallow depression called Eagle Crater. It landed just 16 miles (26 km) from the center of its target zone. One scientist called it an "interplanetary hole in one."

Eagle Crater was formed by a meteorite that slammed into the ground. The impact exposed layers of rock on the sides of the crater. The layers appeared to be sedimentary, formed by water sometime in the planet's distant past. Opportunity investigated the rocks with a microscope. It also used spectrometers that identified chemical elements. (Elements react in unique ways to light. That includes visible light, like we see with our eyes, and invisible light, like microwaves and X-rays.)

Opportunity also found tiny blue-gray rocks shaped like balls. Thousands of them were strewn across the crater floor. Nicknamed "blueberries," they were made of the mineral hematite. It usually forms in the presence of water. Opportunity had discovered more proof of Mars's wet history.

Opportunity discovered "blueberries," small rocks made of hematite, which usually form only in water.

Meanwhile, on the other side of the planet, Spirit's software problems were fixed. It continued exploring the Martian landscape. It used a rock-grinding tool and a microscope to examine the volcanic basalt of the area.

Spirit began a long trip to an area called Columbia Hills (named in honor of the destroyed space shuttle). It climbed hills and found exposed rocks that were probably altered by water, unlike the volcanic basalt in the rover's landing zone.

During its journey, Spirit began losing power. NASA controllers realized that after months of exploring the planet's surface, the rover's solar panels were becoming covered in Martian dust. The fine-grained dust blocked the Sun's rays. Luckily, a dust devil (a small, tornado-like whirlwind) eventually came along and blew much of the debris off the solar panels. The Opportunity rover also had its solar panels cleared by dust devils and windstorms. These occasional cleanings boosted Spirit and Opportunity's power. It was one reason why the rovers were able to explore Mars far longer than expected.

A Martian dust devil photographed by Opportunity.

# THE LONG JOURNEY

Spirit and Opportunity each lasted much longer than scientists had planned. Their main missions were scheduled to last 90 days. In fact, each rover spent many years roaming the Martian surface. Spirit explored many features inside the Gusev Crater basin. It drove partway around the rim of Bonneville Crater, and climbed to the exposed bedrock atop Columbia Hills.

Opportunity began its own long trek after climbing out of Eagle Crater in mid-2004. Its first major stop: Victoria Crater. One-half mile (.8 km) in diameter, the crater had eroded "fingers" around its rim that would be interesting to study. Along the way, Opportunity drove past its own heat shield, which was jettisoned during landing. Nearby was an intact meteorite embedded in the soil. About the size of a basketball, it was named Heat Shield Rock.

Opportunity discovered a meteorite near the rover's discarded heat shield.

Driving across Mars was a slow process for both rovers. They usually ambled over the surface at just 2 feet (.6 m) per minute. On a good day, the rovers might cover a few hundred feet of distance, analyzing rocks and taking stunning panoramic photos of the Martian landscape as they went. Each step in the journey was carefully planned by controllers on Earth. Sometimes, when long stretches of roving were planned, Spirit and Opportunity were allowed to drive by themselves. When the rovers met unexpected obstacles, they drove around them automatically or stopped and radioed home for help.

*Above:* A satellite view of the one-half mile (.8-km) -wide Victoria Crater.
*Below:* Opportunity's ground view photo of one of Victoria Crater's cliffs.

Spirit got stuck in loose sand in 2009.

During winter, the rovers were put into sleep mode at night to conserve energy. Dust gathering on the solar panels reduced their available power. At night, temperatures on Mars often plunged to -140 degrees Fahrenheit (-96° C) or colder. Internal heaters protected the rovers' electronics, but with less power to draw from, the cold eventually took its toll.

In 2009, Spirit's wheels got stuck in sandy soil. Controllers tried for months to find ways to free the rover, but it was no use. Then, on March 22, 2010, Spirit sent its last radio signals to Earth. It had spent more than six years exploring Mars before succumbing to the harsh conditions. During its service, Spirit took more than 128,000 photographs and uncovered more evidence that water had once covered much of the Red Planet.

In 2008, Opportunity left Victoria Crater and began a long journey to Endeavour Crater. Seven miles (11 km) distant, the trip took almost 3 years. Along the way, the rover took many side trips to explore and analyze interesting rocks and craters. It also found more meteorites.

In August 2011, Opportunity reached the rim of Endeavour Crater. This was a much bigger crater than Victoria Crater, measuring about 14 miles (23 km) in diameter. Opportunity has spent years at the rim because of the interesting rocks and bluffs in the area. Many of the rocks that the rover analyzed could only have been formed long ago in the presence of water.

As of this writing, Opportunity has been functioning on Mars for more than 14 years, and has traveled about 28 miles (45 km). Mars's longest-working rover is still exploring the planet's geology and weather. It has taken more than 228,000 breathtaking pictures, and continues to find many surprises on the Red Planet.

A dusty Opportunity rover (below) captures itself and a panoramic view of the huge Endeavour Crater in a 2012 mosaic photo.

# CURIOSITY

NASA's Curiosity is the biggest and most technologically advanced rover to ever land and work on Mars. NASA engineers began planning its mission in the early 2000s. Its most important goal was to discover if Mars ever had the right conditions to support tiny life forms called microbes. It would do this by analyzing the Martian soil, rocks, and air. The rover would be looking especially for organic material. Organics are the chemical building blocks of all life as we know it.

Part of the Mars Science Laboratory mission, the Curiosity rover took more than 7 years to plan, build, and test. About the size of a small car, the rover has six wide wheels with a rocker-bogie suspension. That is similar to its predecessor rovers Spirit, Opportunity, and Sojourner. It allows Curiosity to roll over tall obstacles and climb steep hills. Unlike those previous rovers, however, Curiosity was built much bigger so that it can hold more scientific instruments. The rover measures 10 feet (3 m) long, 9 feet (2.7 m) wide, and 7 feet (2.1 m) high. It weighs nearly 1 ton, tipping the scales at 1,982 pounds (899 kg). It is about twice as long and 5 times as heavy as either the Spirit or Opportunity rovers.

Curiosity is the largest rover sent to Mars to date. It is about the size of a small car.

## MARS CURIOSITY ROVER

| | | | |
|---|---|---|---|
| Mission: | Mars rover | Mars Touchdown: | August 6, 2012 |
| Launch: | November 26, 2011 | Mission End: | Continuing |
| Launch Vehicle: | Atlas V | Spacecraft weight (mass) rover only: | 1,982 pounds (899 kg) |

Previous Martian rovers got their power from solar panels. However, dust often gathered on the flat panels. That reduced the amount of sunlight that could be used to generate electricity. Instead of solar panels, Curiosity has a radioisotope power system. It uses the heat generated by radioactive plutonium-238 and converts it to electricity. It is very dependable, and provides more than enough power for roaming across the Martian landscape and for all the rover's scientific instruments.

Two identical computers control Curiosity. If one computer crashes or has problems, the backup computer takes over. Curiosity can directly communicate by radio with controllers on Earth. It can also send data to satellites orbiting Mars, which then relay the messages to Earth.

Curiosity's robotic arm works at Mars's Yellowknife Bay.

Curiosity bristles with scientific equipment. It has spectrometers and lasers that analyze the chemical elements in rock, soil, and air samples. It has a radiation detector. It also has 17 cameras. Some

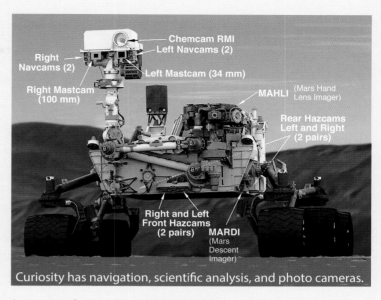

Chemcam RMI
Left Navcams (2)
Right Navcams (2)
Left Mastcam (34 mm)
Right Mastcam (100 mm)
MAHLI (Mars Hand Lens Imager)
Rear Hazcams Left and Right (2 pairs)
Right and Left Front Hazcams (2 pairs)
MARDI (Mars Descent Imager)

Curiosity has navigation, scientific analysis, and photo cameras.

take high-resolution photos of the Martian landscape, while others help avoid hazards while roaming. Several are mounted on a tall mast that extends several feet upward.

The rover is also equipped with a 6.9-foot (2.1-m) -long robotic arm. There are several instruments on the end of the arm. They include a close-up camera, X-ray spectrometer, drill, rock-cleaning brush, and a scoop. After drilling .6-inch (1.5-cm) -wide holes in rocks or soil, the arm gathers up the powdered samples and moves them to chemistry labs inside the rover.

# SEVEN MINUTES OF TERROR

Curiosity launched atop a Delta V rocket on November 26, 2011.

The Curiosity rover was carried to Mars aboard the Mars Science Laboratory (MSL) spacecraft. The MSL was equipped with computers, rockets, and fuel. A 14.8-foot (4.5-m) heat shield would protect the rover during the trip through the Martian atmosphere, and a large parachute would help slow its speed. The MSL was assembled at NASA's Jet Propulsion Laboratory in Pasadena, California.

The MSL spacecraft, with Curiosity aboard, launched from Florida's Cape Canaveral Air Force Station on November 26, 2011. It was carried into space by a powerful Atlas V rocket. During its eight-month trip to Mars, the spacecraft travelled about 352 million miles (566 million km).

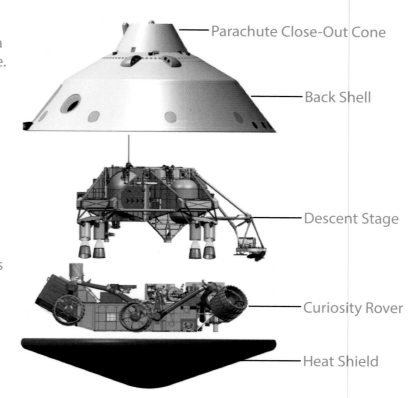

Curiosity was nestled inside a protective cone. Once through Mars's outer atmosphere, the automatic landing equipment had to work flawlessly in order for the rover to reach the Red Planet's surface safely.

Parachute Close-Out Cone

Back Shell

Descent Stage

Curiosity Rover

Heat Shield

Curiosity landed on Mars on August 6, 2012. Getting to the planet's surface was a tense ordeal. Because of the millions of miles of distance between the two planets, Curiosity had to land automatically. Everything had to work just right, and be perfectly timed. If any one piece of equipment failed, the spacecraft would crash.

It would take seven minutes for the spacecraft to travel from the top of the atmosphere to the surface. It took 14 long minutes for the rover's radio signals to reach Earth. For that reason, by the time NASA scientists got word that Curiosity had entered the top of the atmosphere, the rover would have already landed safely on Mars, or slammed into the rocky ground and been destroyed. NASA called this the "seven minutes of terror."

About 78 miles
(126 km) above
Mars's surface,
the spacecraft
slammed into the
atmosphere. Traveling
about 13,000 miles per
hour (20,921 kph), the friction
of speeding through the air caused
the heat shield to reach 3,800 degrees
Fahrenheit (2,093° C). Inside, Curiosity stayed
cool at about 50 degrees Fahrenheit (10° C).

The spacecraft fired small rockets to guide it to its landing
zone. About 7 miles (11 km) above the ground, the spacecraft's
speed dropped to 900 miles per hour (1,448 kph). Soon, a large
parachute billowed out, and the heat shield popped off.

Radar helped the spacecraft judge the distance to the surface.
About one mile (1.6 km) up, the top shell and parachute were
ejected, and the spacecraft went into free fall, traveling 170 miles
per hour (274 kph). Eight retrorockets fired, slowing the descent. In
the final few seconds, the spacecraft came to a near-hover.

Unlike previous rovers, Curiosity was too heavy to land safely using airbags to cushion the impact. Instead, it used a radical new method called a "sky crane." The rover was lowered from the upper-stage spacecraft to the ground by three 21-foot (6.4-m) -long nylon ropes. This kept the rover far away from the spacecraft's retrorockets. Otherwise, they would have stirred up dust and rocks on the Martian surface, which could have harmed the rover.

After Curiosity was safely on the ground, the ropes were cut and the upper stage flew off. It intentionally crashed about 500 feet (152 m) away so it wouldn't harm the rover. Curiosity signaled its controllers on Earth: it was ready to begin its mission.

Once the Curiosity rover was safely lowered to the ground, the sky crane ropes were cut free and the upper-stage spacecraft flew off. It intentionally crashed about 500 feet (152 m) away so that it couldn't harm the rover.

# EXPLORING GALE CRATER

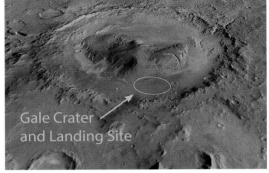

Gale Crater and Landing Site

Curiosity made an almost pinpoint landing inside Gale Crater, in the Elysium Planitia region of Mars. The landing site was named Bradbury Landing, in honor of author Ray Bradbury. Gale Crater was chosen as a landing site because there is evidence that ancient waterways once flowed there. A meteorite slammed into Mars billions of years ago, forming the 100-mile (161-km) -diameter crater. It later filled with water. Over millions of years, layers of sediment and erosion formed a large bulge that rises 18,000 feet (5,486 m) in the middle of the crater, called Mount Sharp. Now that water has vanished from the surface of Mars, scientists hope that Curiosity will uncover clues about the planet's watery past.

Curiosity immediately began sending home spectacular high-resolution photographs of its surroundings. Within a few days, NASA controllers sent the rover instructions to begin exploring the area. It zapped nearby rocks with a laser and analyzed the vapor with a spectrometer to figure out their type. It also collected many soil and bedrock samples with its drill and scoop.

In July 2013, Curiosity began a long journey to the base of Mount Sharp. Along the way, it took jaw-dropping images of the Red Planet, and studied many interesting rocks. It arrived at the base of Mount Sharp in September 2014.

In 2012, Curiosity worked at a spot inside Gale Crater. This mosaic image shows scoop marks in the sand (left), rover tracks, and Mount Sharp rising on the right.

In June 2018, NASA announced that Curiosity had discovered organic molecules on the lower slopes of Mount Sharp. They were preserved inside three-billion-year-old sedimentary mudstone (made from muds and clays). The chemistry lab inside Curiosity heated powdered rock samples to 932 degrees Fahrenheit (500° C). This released

Curiosity drilled a .6-inch (1.5 cm) -wide hole in Martian rock. The rover's work has uncovered organic molecules on Mars.

chemicals in the form of gas so they could be analyzed. Organic molecules contain carbon atoms, and are the basic building blocks of living creatures, including microbes.

Curiosity also discovered methane gas in the Martian air. The rover "breathes" the Martian atmosphere through two intake valves on its side and analyzes it. Scientists discovered that the levels of methane increase seasonally. Methane is often found as a byproduct of living organisms. Scientists wonder if the increasing methane is coming from active colonies of underground microbes during the warmer summer months.

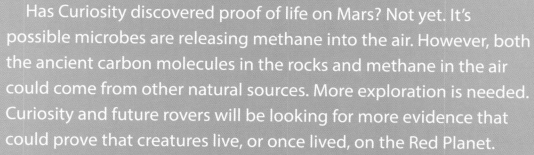

Has Curiosity discovered proof of life on Mars? Not yet. It's possible microbes are releasing methane into the air. However, both the ancient carbon molecules in the rocks and methane in the air could come from other natural sources. More exploration is needed. Curiosity and future rovers will be looking for more evidence that could prove that creatures live, or once lived, on the Red Planet.

The Curiosity rover was built to last two years, but its mission has lasted far longer. As of late 2018, it has been exploring Mars for more than three times its expected life span. It has survived several frigid Martian winters and traveled more than 11 miles (17.7 km) across the alien landscape. With any luck, it will continue its exploration for many years to come.

Although dusty and showing signs of wear on its wheels, Curiosity continues to explore Mars.

# NEXT-GENERATION ROVERS

Every two years, Earth and Mars are closest together in their orbits, which is the best time to send spacecraft. The next "launch window" happens in 2020. Both NASA and the European Space Agency (ESA) plan to launch new rovers to Mars during that time.

The Mars 2020 rover will look similar to the Curiosity rover. It will also use the same kind of sky crane landing system. Its mission will be to continue the search for potential signs of life on Mars. It will collect rock samples that may someday be returned to science labs on Earth. The rover will test a way to produce oxygen from the Martian air, and help identify possible underground water. It will have 22 cameras, and a microphone to capture sounds from Mars. The rover will also carry a unique passenger: Mars Helicopter Scout. This small, solar-powered drone will help find targets for the rover to study.

NASA's Mars 2020 rover will explore the Red Planet with the Mars Helicopter Scout.

The ESA's ExoMars rover looks similar to NASA's Spirit and Opportunity rovers. Its main mission will be to find signs of life on Mars. Its science equipment includes ground-penetrating radar, advanced spectrometers for analyzing rocks, and chemistry labs to look for organic molecules. Its drill can burrow almost 7 feet (2.1 m) underground to find unspoiled rock core samples.

More rovers and orbiters are planned for 2022 and beyond. If all goes according to plan, Mars will have a fleet of robotic spacecraft exploring its surface. The data gathered by these scientific marvels will pave the way for human exploration of the Red Planet in the coming decades.

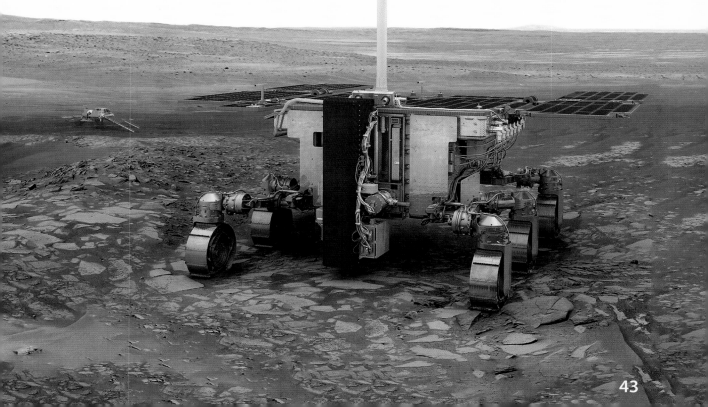

The European Space Agency's ExoMars rover is scheduled to launch in July 2020.

# TIMELINE

Mars 2 & 3 Lander & Prop-M Rover

**November 27, 1971**—Mars 2 (USSR) lander crashes. It becomes the first human object to reach the surface of Mars.

**December 2, 1971**—Mars 3 (USSR) lander successfully lands on Mars. However, instruments fail 20 seconds after landing. The Prop-M rover never makes it to the Mars surface.

Pathfinder Launch

**December 4, 1996**—Mars Pathfinder (USA) spacecraft, with Sojourner rover aboard, lifts off from Florida's Cape Canaveral Air Force Station.

**July 4, 1997**—Mars Pathfinder lands safely on Mars. Accompanying Sojourner rover successfully deployed to the Martian surface. Lander renamed Carl Sagan Memorial Station.

Pathfinder & Sojourner

**September 27, 1997**—Radio communications from Pathfinder and Sojourner (USA) cease. They probably fell victim to the extreme cold temperatures on Mars.

Spirit Launch     Opportunity Launch

**June 10, 2003**—Spirit (USA) rover lifts off from Cape Canaveral.

**July 7, 2003**—Opportunity (USA) rover lifts off from Cape Canaveral.

Spirit & Opportunity

**January 4, 2004**—Spirit rover lands safely on Mars.

**January 25, 2004**—Opportunity rover lands safely on Mars.

Spirit Stuck in the Sand

**March 22, 2010**—Spirit sends its last radio signals to Earth. After being stuck in deep sand for months, it probably succumbed to the harsh Martian weather conditions.

Curiosity Launch

**November 26, 2011**—Mars Science Laboratory (USA), with the Curiosity rover aboard, takes off from Cape Canaveral.

Curiosity Sky Crane Landing

**August 6, 2012**—Curiosity rover touches down on Mars using a unique and daring "sky crane" landing technique.

Curiosity

**June 2018**—NASA announces that Curiosity has discovered organic molecules inside ancient Martian rocks, and methane in the air that increases in the warmer summer months. Both may be signs of microbial life on Mars, but further investigations are needed.

Mars 2020 Rover

**2020**—NASA's next-generation robotic explorer, called the Mars 2020 rover, plus the European Space Agency's ExoMars rover, are scheduled to lift off. If all goes well, both rovers should land on Mars in early 2021.

ExoMars

# GLOSSARY

**COLUMBIA HILLS**

A range of small hills inside Gusev Crater. The Spirit rover explored the area for several years during its mission. The range is named after the destroyed space shuttle Columbia. The seven peaks are named after the astronauts who died during the disaster in 2003.

**EUROPEAN SPACE AGENCY (ESA)**

A space agency, like NASA, that builds and flies spacecraft that explore the solar system. Its headquarters is in Paris, France. As of 2018, there are 22 countries that are members of the ESA.

**GALE CRATER**

Gale Crater is the large crater where the Curiosity rover landed. It is named after Walter Frederick Gale (1865-1945), an Australian amateur astronomer who studied Mars in the late 1800s. He also discovered several new comets.

**GUSEV CRATER**

A 103-mile (166-km) -diameter crater in the Aeolis region of Mars. Explored by the Spirit rover, Gusev Crater is named after Russian astronomer Matvei Gusev (1826-1866), who was a pioneer of astrophotography.

**JET PROPULSION LABORATORY (JPL)**

A NASA-owned research center based in Pasadena, California. It is managed for NASA by the California Institute of Technology (Caltech). JPL's main mission is to plan and construct robotic spacecraft that explore space and our solar system, including Mars.

**MICROBE**

Small life-forms (microorganisms), such as bacteria, fungi, or viruses. The Curiosity rover's main mission was to explore whether Mars could be home to microbial life in its distant past.

### National Aeronautics and Space Administration (NASA)

A United States government space agency started in 1958. NASA's goals include space exploration, as well as increasing people's understanding of Earth, our solar system, and the universe.

### Sedimentary

Rock that is formed by sediments (tiny particles of rocks carried by water) that collect and press together over thousands or millions of years. Sandstone is a sedimentary rock.

### Solar Flare

A sudden increase in Sun activity. These bright flashes cause electrons, ions, and other electromagnetic energy to be violently ejected into space.

### Soviet Union

A former country that included a union of Russia and several other communist republics. It was formed in 1922 and existed until 1991.

### Spectrometer

A spectrometer is a recording device that lets scientists collect data about light (the electromagnetic spectrum) that humans can't see, such as gamma rays, X-rays, microwaves, and radio waves. Light that humans can see is called "visible light." It is just a small part of the entire electromagnetic spectrum.

# ONLINE RESOURCES

**Booklinks**
NONFICTION NETWORK
FREE! ONLINE NONFICTION RESOURCES

To learn more about Mars rovers, visit abdobooklinks.com. These links are routinely monitored and updated to provide the most current information available.

# INDEX